First World War
and Army of Occupation
War Diary
France, Belgium and Germany

66 DIVISION
Divisional Troops
Royal Army Medical Corps
2/3 East Lancashire Field Ambulance
13 September 1915 - 26 February 1916

WO95/3132/1

The Naval & Military Press Ltd
www.nmarchive.com
Published in association with The National Archives

Published by

The Naval & Military Press Ltd

Unit 10 Ridgewood Industrial Park,

Uckfield, East Sussex,

TN22 5QE England

Tel: +44 (0) 1825 749494

www.naval-military-press.com

www.nmarchive.com

This diary has been reprinted in facsimile from the original. Any imperfections are inevitably reproduced and the quality may fall short of modern type and cartographic standards.

© **Crown Copyright**
Images reproduced by permission of The National Archives, London, England, 2015.

Contents

Document type	Place/Title	Date From	Date To
Heading	WO95/3132/1		
Heading	66 Div Troops 2/3 East Lancs Fld Amb 1915 Sep-1916 Feb		
Miscellaneous	66th (East Lancashire) Division	31/08/1915	31/08/1915
War Diary	Fear Pottage	13/09/1915	22/09/1915
War Diary	East Grinstead	23/09/1915	23/09/1915
War Diary	Tonbridge	24/09/1915	24/09/1915
War Diary	Burham	28/09/1915	28/09/1915
War Diary	Burham Camp Nr. Eccles Kent	28/09/1915	28/09/1915
War Diary	Burham Nr. Eccles	01/10/1915	01/10/1915
War Diary	Maidstone	02/10/1915	17/10/1915
War Diary	Crowborough Sussex	22/10/1915	22/10/1915
War Diary	Burham	24/10/1915	27/10/1915
War Diary	Crowborough Sussex	29/10/1915	29/10/1915
War Diary	Burham	30/10/1915	30/10/1915
War Diary	Crowborough	31/10/1915	31/10/1915
War Diary	Crowborough	14/12/1915	28/12/1915
War Diary	Crowborough Sussex	21/01/1916	28/01/1916
Heading	War Diary of 2/3rd East Lancashire Field Ambulance From 1st February 1916 To 29th Feby 1916 Volume		
War Diary	Crowborough Sussex	02/02/1916	26/02/1916

WO 95/3132/1

66 DIV TROOPS

2/3 EAST LANCS FLD AMB

1915 SEP — 1916 FEB

3018

66th. (East Lancashire) Division.

Unit.	2/3rd. East Lancashire Field Ambulance.
Brigade.	198th. (East Lancs.) Infantry Brigade.
Division.	66th. (East Lancs.) Division.
Mobilization Centre.	RAMC.T.F.Depot, Upper Chorlton Road, Manchester.
Temporary War Station.	Peas Pottage, Near Crawley, Sussex.
Stations occupied.	Littleborough, Lancashire) as details of 1/3rd.
	Croxteth Park, West Derby, Lancs.) East Lancs. Fld. Amb..
	Southport, Lancashire.) as 2/3rd. East Lancs.
	Lindfield. Sussex.) Field Ambulance.
(a) Mobilization.	1st. Line Unit mobilized 5th. August 1915.
(b) Concentration at War Station.	Attached to 198th. Infantry Brigade.
(c) Organisation for defence.	The strength of the Unit, both as regards Officers and Men is still very low in consequence of drafts to the 1st. Line Unit serving with the Mediterranean Expeditionary Force.
(d) Training.	Training is progressing as far as possible having regard to the facts set forth under para. (c) The training of the Transport has been facilitated by the advent of several more horses and full advantage is being taken of the animals and equipment now available.
(e) Discipline.	Verygood.
(f) Administration.	
1. Medical Services.	Medical and Surgical Stores are still incomplete.
2. Vet. Services.	Local Veterinary Services rendered by Civilian Veterinary Surgeon appointed by Brigade.
3. Supply Services.	---
4. Transport Services	Shortage of heavy draught horses and Transport vehicles.
5. Ordnance Service.	---
6. Billeting&Hutting.	This Unit is under canvas and all arrangemnets are satisfactory.
7. Channels of Correspondence.)	Through A.D.M.S., 66th. (East Lancs.) Division, Crowborough. Restricted Postal Services.
8. Range construction.	Nil.
9. Supply of Remounts.	---
(g) Reorganisation of T.F. into Home and Imperial Service.)	All ranks have undertaken the Imperial Service obligation.
(h) Preparation of T.F. for Imperial Service.	Every opportunity is taken to train the Unit as far as possible, in accordance with the principles laid down and recommended by notes from the Fronts.

1/3 East Lancs Field Amb

WAR DIARY
or
INTELLIGENCE SUMMARY.
(Erase heading not required.)

Army Form C. 2118.

Instructions regarding War Diaries and Intelligence Summaries are contained in F. S. Regs., Part II. and the Staff Manual respectively. Title pages will be prepared in manuscript.

Place	Date	Hour	Summary of Events and Information	Remarks and references to Appendices
Pens Cottage	13/9/15	9.0 am	Fld. Amb. accompanies 198th Inf. Bde. on march by following route :— Pens Cottage, Barncamp, The Goldings, Doomsday Green, Horsham, Roffey, Colgate, Pens Cottage.	
Pens Cottage	19/9/15	9.0 am	Fld. Amb. accompanies 198th Inf. Bde. on march by following route :— Crawley, Ifield Park, Gate Inn, Lambs Green, Faygate, Colgate, Pens Cottage.	
Pens Cottage	20/9/15	7.0 am	Fld. Amb. accompanies 198th Inf. Bde. on march by following route :— Pens Cottage, Handcross, High Beeches, Brook Side, Staplefield Place, Handcross, Pens Cottage.	
Pens Cottage	22/9/15	7.0 am	Fld. Ambulance accompanies 198th Inf. Bde. on change of station from Pens Cottage to Burham Camp, Nr. Eccles, Kent. Brigade moves by road. Billeted at East Grinstead at night.	198th Inf. Bde. Order No. Order 295-6-7 of Sept. 21st 22nd 23rd respectively
East Grinstead	23/9/15		Brigade continues march to New Station. Billeted at Tonbridge for night.	
Tonbridge	24/9/15		Brigade continues march to New Station and arrives Burham Camp.	
Burham	25/9/15	8.0 am	50 men of Field Ambulance detailed to assist Brigade on Entrenching Operation connected with London Defences, whilst at this station.	
Burham	26/9/15	1.0 pm	Inspection of Camp by G.O.C. and A.D.M.S. 66th (East Lancs) Division.	198th Bde Order

Burham Camp.
Nr. Eccles.
Kent.
26.9.15

W. Attwell Capt.
for Officer Commanding
1/3 East Lancs. Field Amb.

WAR DIARY or INTELLIGENCE SUMMARY

Army Form C. 2118.

2/3 Eas Lancs field Amb

(Erase heading not required.)

Instructions regarding War Diaries and Intelligence Summaries are contained in F.S. Regs., Part II. and the Staff Manual respectively. Title pages will be prepared in manuscript.

Place	Date	Hour	Summary of Events and Information	Remarks and references to Appendices
BURHAM NR. ECCLES. MAIDSTONE	1/10/15		"Retreat" to be sounded at 5 pm.	198th Inf Bde Ordrs 43 1/10/15 66th East Lancs
	2/10/15		Rev. Father M. BECKETT (Roman Catholic Chaplain) attached to Unit for Billeting and Rations	Distr Ordrs 1502 2/14/10/15
"	6/10/15	4.0pm	Inspection of men by representative of Ministry of Munitions.	66th (East Lancs)
"	13/10/15		Orders re. shooting of Carrier Pigeons on passage published in Regimental Orders	Div. Order 9-10-15
"	15/10/15	12 noon	Inspection of Camp by A.D.M.S. 66th (East Lancs) Divn	
"	16/10/15		Epidemic of Scabies detected in Battalion of 198th Infantry Brigade and steps at once taken to combat it (Isolation Hospital Established, arrangement made with Maidstone and Chatham Union for storing of Kits, bedding, clothes etc.)	
"	19/10/15	12 noon	Transport of Field Ambulance inspected by Officer Commanding 198th Infantry Bde.	
CROWBOROUGH SUSSEX	22/10/15		Draft of 62 recruits arrive at Crowborough from Administration Centre R.A.M.C. (T.F.) Depôt MANCHESTER and await, under command of Capt. E.G. Wray, arrival of Unit from Burham.	
BURHAM	27/10/15	12 noon	Transport of Field Ambulance inspected by Officer Commanding 198th Inf. Bde.	
"	27/10/15		Epidemic of Scabies officially stamped out	
CROWBOROUGH SUSSEX	29/10/15		Further draft of 38 recruits from Administration Centre Manchester	
BURHAM	30/10/15	8.0 am	Field Ambulance accompanies 2/9th and 2/10th Batt. Manchester Regt. by road to rest station at CROWBOROUGH (billets at TONBRIDGE for night	
CROWBOROUGH	31/10/15	1.0 pm	Unit arrives at New Station and occupies hutments Brackets 17, 2/24 East Lancs Field Amb	
Crowborough 3/10/15				Col E Ferguson Captain Comg

Army Form C. 2118.

1315

WAR DIARY 2/3 Gloucestershire Club
or
INTELLIGENCE SUMMARY
(Erase heading not required.)

Instructions regarding War Diaries and Intelligence Summaries are contained in F.S. Regs., Part II. and the Staff Manual respectively. Title pages will be prepared in manuscript.

Place	Date	Hour	Summary of Events and Information	Remarks and references to Appendices
CROMBOROUGH. 30ᵗʰ Novʳ 1915.			"NIL" Report for month of NOVEMBER 1915.	F.C. Prestwich Capt. and Act. Adjutant, 2/3rd East Lancs. Field Amb.
				C B Terpum Capt. Officer Commanding, 2/3 East Lancs. Field Amb.

WAR DIARY 2/3 Lancashire Cmb
or
INTELLIGENCE SUMMARY.

Army Form C. 2118.

1915

(Erase heading not required.)

Place	Date	Hour	Summary of Events and Information	Remarks and references to Appendices
			NIL REPORT for month of DECEMBER 1915	F.C. Prestwich Lieutenant Act. Adjutant, 2/3rd East Lancs. Field Amb.
Crosbos	14/12/15		Inspection of Field Ambulances on route march to Mayfield by A.D.C. + D.D.M.S 66"(2nd Lancs.) Division - Satisfactory	
	29/12/15		Transport of ambulance transferred to A.S.C. - authority W.O. Letter 121/Medicine/1427 (2M,S) dated 22/9/15	

Goodenough Lund
Lieut Colonel
3rd December 1915

Cuthbertson Lynas
Officer Commanding
2/3rd East Lancs. F.H. Amb.

Army Form C. 2118.

WAR DIARY 2/3 E Lancs Field Amb
or
INTELLIGENCE SUMMARY.
(Erase heading not required.)

Instructions regarding War Diaries and Intelligence Summaries are contained in F. S. Regs., Part II. and the Staff Manual respectively. Title pages will be prepared in manuscript.

Place	Date	Hour	Summary of Events and Information	Remarks and references to Appendices
Cegrbornays Suarez	1916. 27th Jan.	10.30 a.m.	Inspection by A.D.M.S. Central Force on Sunday Standing Present :- Officers 7, N.C.Os and Men 155, Horses 34, Vehicles 12.	J.N.
	27th Jan		Extract of report of Surgeon General Bulling P.A.M.S. Central Force, dated 26th Jany 1916, received through A.D.M.S. 66th (East Lancs) Division :- "I saw the units on parade and was satisfied with the way in which they acquitted themselves."	J.N.
	28th Jan		Inspection of field ambulance marching to trenches Sept.D.M.S. He expressed satisfaction	Weymouth

Thos Noel
Major Lanc. C.J.
Officer Commanding,
2/3 East Lancs. Field Amb.
Div.

CONFIDENTIAL.

WAR DIARY

of

2/3rd. EAST LANCASHIRE FIELD AMBULANCE

FROM 1st. February 1916 to 29th. Feby. 1916.

VOLUME ~~II.~~ 1

Army Form C.2118.

WAR DIARY
or
INTELLIGENCE SUMMARY
(Erase heading not required.)

Instructions regarding War Diaries and Intelligence Summaries are contained in F.S. Regs., Part II. and the Staff Manual respectively. Title pages will be prepared in manuscript.

Place	Date	Hour	Summary of Events and Information	Remarks and references to Appendices
CROWBOROUGH SUSSEX.	2/2/16	12 noon	Concentration and Inspection by A.D.S.T., SECOND ARMY, CENTRAL FORCE, of Divisional Transport at HARTFIELD, 7 miles from HEADQUARTERS, 2/3RD EAST LANCASHIRE FIELD AMBULANCE, consisted of COMMANDING OFFICER, TRANSPORT OFFICER, N.C.Os 3, MEN 29, HORSES 32, AMBULANCE WAGONS 2, G.S. WAGONS 5, LIMBERED G.S. 3, WATERCARTS 3, MALTESE CART 1, 5 A.S.C. MEN from No. 544 COMPANY, 66TH (EAST LANCS.) DIVISIONAL TRAIN attached to this Unit for all purposes.	F.G.P. F.G.P.
CROWBOROUGH SUSSEX.	5/2/16		Extract from notes on the Inspection by OFFICER COMMANDING 66TH (EAST LANCS) of 2/2/16.	F.G.P.
CROWBOROUGH SUSSEX.	8/2/16		DIVISIONAL TRAIN 8/2/16 "Well turned out in every respect." Medical and Surgical Equipment for one Section, transferred to 2/3RD EAST LANCASHIRE FIELD AMBULANCE from 2/3RD HOME COUNTIES FIELD AMBULANCE.	F.G.P.
CROWBOROUGH SUSSEX.	19/2/16			F.G.P.
CROWBOROUGH SUSSEX.	26/2/16		ONE R.A.M.C. TRANSPORT PERSONNEL transferred to No. 544 COMPANY, 66TH (EAST LANCS) DIVISIONAL TRAIN, and attached to the 2/3RD EAST LANCASHIRE FIELD AMBULANCE, for all purposes. 26/2/16.	F.G.P.

[signature]
Major
Officer Commanding
2/3rd East Lancs...

T2134. Wt. W708—776. 500000. 4/15. Sir J. C. & S.

www.ingramcontent.com/pod-product-compliance
Lightning Source LLC
Chambersburg PA
CBHW081518160426
43193CB00014B/2725